The Sun, the Wind and the Rain

Lisa Westberg Peters

Illustrated by Ted Rand

Henry Holt and Company · New York

Henry Holt and Company, LLC
Publishers since 1866
175 Fifth Avenue
New York, New York 10010
www.henryholtchildrensbooks.com

Library of Congress Cataloging-in-Publication Data
Peters, Lisa Westberg.
The sun, the wind and the rain.
Summary: Presents side-by-side narration of the earth's making of a
mountain, shaping it with sun, wind, and rain, and a child's efforts at the
beach to make a tall sand mountain which is also affected by the elements.
1. Science—Juvenile literature.   2. Nature—Juvenile literature.
[1. Mountains.   2. Nature.]   I. Rand, Ted, ill.   II. Title.
Q163.P46   1988   551.4′32   87-23808

ISBN-13: 978-0-8050-1481-5 / ISBN-10: 0-8050-1481-0
First published in hardcover in 1988 by Henry Holt and Company
First paperback edition—1990
Printed in China
25   24   23   22   21   20   19   18

For Dave, Emily and Anna

This is the story of two mountains. The earth made one.

Elizabeth in her yellow sun hat made the other.

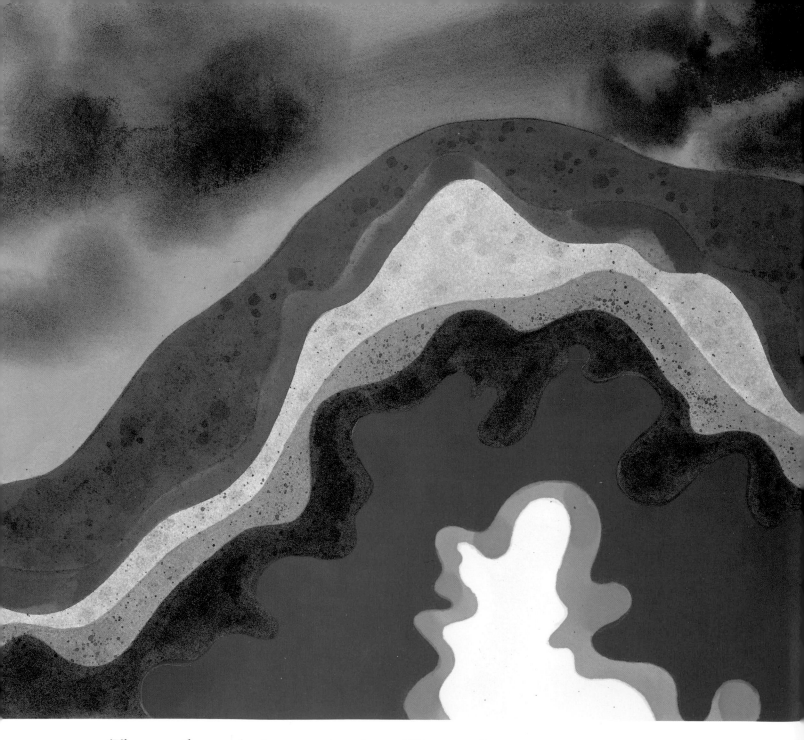

The earth made its mountain millions of years ago.
It began as a pool underground, first fiery hot and soft,
then cold and rock-hard.

Elizabeth made hers on the beach today with bucketsful of wet sand.

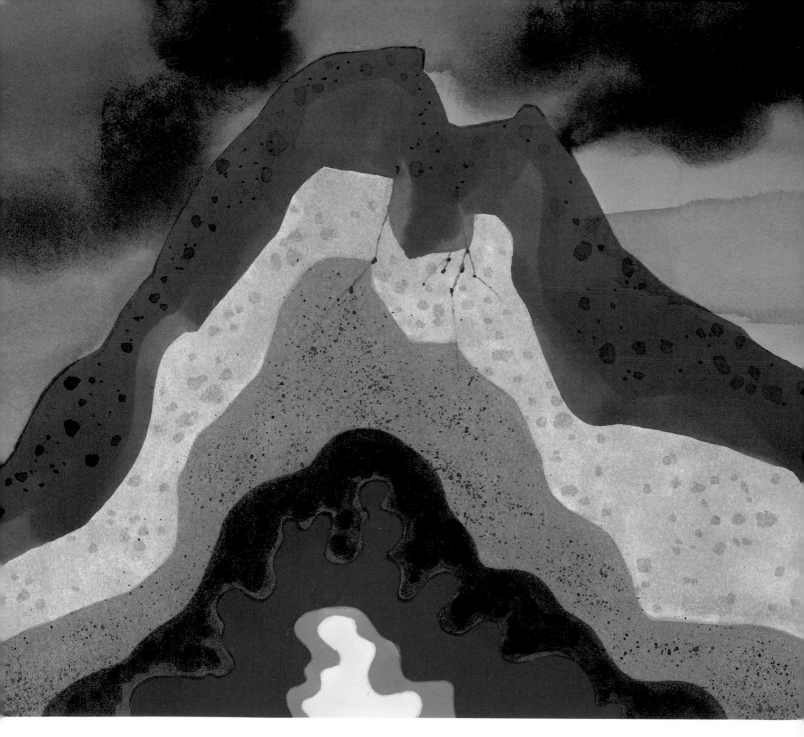

Eons passed. The earth cracked and shifted until the rock of its mountain slowly rose.

Elizabeth quickly piled her sand high. She patted it smooth all the way around.

The earth mountain sparkled against the sky. Furry animals
walked in its lush green valleys.

Elizabeth's mountain stood almost as tall as she, with
twigs for trees and pebbles for animals. Elizabeth was proud
of her fine sand mountain.

The sun beat down, day after day, year after year,
on the earth mountain's sharp peaks. The wind howled through
its canyons.

Elizabeth's mountain baked in the afternoon heat.
The breeze loosened a few grains of sand and blew them
into Elizabeth's eyes and hair.

Countless rainstorms pounded the earth mountain.
The water seeped into its rocks, making them crumble,
then tumble into small streams.

An afternoon shower blew in suddenly and Elizabeth watched
as the water began to destroy the mountain she had worked so
hard to build. Her tears fell as freely as the rain.

The small streams rushed together to become a raging river. The river gouged a deep valley. It ground the earth mountain's rough rocks into smooth pebbles.

Elizabeth could see the rain carving little valleys into
her mountain. Tiny rivers carried the sand down the beach.

As the river flowed away from the earth mountain, it ground pebbles into sand and dumped the sand on a broad plain. Then it emptied into the sea.

Elizabeth saw the sand from her mountain spread silently
into small fans. She wiped away her tears.

In just a blink of earth time, the earth mountain traded rocks for sand, jagged peaks for flat layers.

After a few minutes, the shower was over.
Elizabeth's mountain was just a bump on the beach.

The thick and heavy layers of sand sank down, down, down
into the earth until they were squeezed into layers of sandstone.

Elizabeth scooped up a handful of sand from one of the small fans on the beach. She smiled. It was wet and hard—just right. This time she hurried, for the sun was dropping in the sky.

The earth cracked and shifted again. Bending and breaking,
the sandstone layers slowly rose to become a new mountain.

Elizabeth finished her new sand mountain. She brushed
sand off her hands, picked up her bucket, and walked back up
the beach.

Elizabeth is walking on the new earth mountain.
She steps carefully up the steep path from the beach.

When she stops to rest, she sees a smooth mound of sand
far below. It looks very small.

As she turns to leave, Elizabeth reaches out to touch
the sandstone wall. Tiny grains of sand fall on her shoulders.

She brushes them off and watches them fall to the ground,
where they will stay for just a while . . .

in the sun, the wind and the rain.

A Note About the Book

Lisa Westberg Peters wrote *The Sun, the Wind and the Rain* while she was living in Seattle, Washington, where, she writes, "I was lucky enough to take some good geology courses and several unforgettable trips into the mountains. I was inspired to try to introduce geological concepts to the very young. The story began in the office of Dr. Richard Conway, professor of chemistry and geology at Shoreline Community College in Seattle. I asked him if he knew of a nice and tidy local geological event that would demonstrate the point I was trying to make, that is, the impermanence of mountains and the notion that new mountains are sometimes made of the stuff of old mountains.

"He suggested the Chuckanut Formation in northwestern Washington state. Much of the Chuckanut began as granite mountains, which rivers wore down and deposited in very thick sandstone beds. The beds have since risen and are now exposed in several spots in the foothills of the Cascades. The most scenic outcrop is along the Chuckanut Drive south of Bellingham, Washington. The road twists and turns, with northern Puget Sound beaches below it and Chuckanut Mountain towering above. My family and I collected a few rock samples along that drive and one of those rocks moved with us back to Minnesota and sits on top of a bookshelf in our house.

"While I used many sources of information, the most useful for this story were Dr. Conway, Samuel Johnson's 1983 scientific paper describing the Chuckanut Formation (which appeared in the *Canadian Journal of Earth Science,* Vol. 21, 1984), and the formation itself."

Ms. Peters did not sell her story until she had moved to Minnesota. It was only a happy coincidence that Ted Rand, a Seattle artist, was chosen to illustrate the book. He, too, consulted Dr. Conway—about the technical details in the illustrations—and has, according to the author, depicted the very beach she had in mind, right down to the color and consistency of the sand.